Music Activities & More for Teaching DBT Skills and Enhancing Any Therapy

EVEN FOR THE NON-MUSICIAN

Deborah Spiegel MT-BC

authorHOUSE®

D1211167

AuthorHouse™
1663 Liberty Drive
Bloomington, IN 47403
www.authorhouse.com
Phone: 1-800-839-8640

First published by AuthorHouse 3/30/2010

ISBN: 978-1-4490-9660-1 (sc)
ISBN: 978-1-4490-9662-5 (e)

Library of Congress Control Number: 2010904311

Printed in the United States of America
Bloomington, Indiana

This book is printed on acid-free paper.

TABLE OF CONTENTS

ABOUT THE AUTHOR

ABOUT THE AUTHOR

Deborah Spiegel, MT-BC is a Board- Certified Music Therapist who has been in the field for over 25 years. She currently works at a mental health facility providing music therapy group and individual sessions for people of all ages. She is a member of a multi-disciplinary treatment team and an integral member of a DBT (Dialectical Behavioral Therapy) based milieu.

As a DBT skills group leader and a DBT homework group leader, Deborah uses original songs that reinforce and teach the skills through music, both in music therapy groups and in DBT groups. She often works individually with clients and takes the material they give her about their lives and hopes and writes a song for them. Thus, the clients feel validated as they are and at the same time encouraged to change which is a DBT goal. They say things like "This song helps me so much! It reminds me to use my skills!"

Some of Deborah's original songs that reinforce DBT skills are recorded on a CD called *"You'll. Make It Through the Rain"* which is a companion to this book

One unique qualification that Deborah Spiegel has is certification in clinical hypnotherapy which adds depth to her guided imagery sessions. She helps people develop inner resources for love, nurturing, and success when their outer resources are bleak and few. She help people to create inner harmony, overcome addictions, change behavioral patterns, gain clarity, overcome traumatic experiences, relax, experience richer relationships, gain confidence, end self-sabotage, be a success, feel greater self love, and more. The best part is that the process gives the recipients tools to help them bring about real, lasting and nourishing changes in their own lives.   She conducts imagery sessions in person or over the telephone in her private practice and she especially likes working with youth.

Deborah makes professional presentations at seminars and workshops and conducts in-service training on:

- the use of therapeutic music activities that can be integrated into any treatment or educational program
- how to use music to reinforce and teach DBT skills
- how to use her original songs therapeutically
- an experiential introduction to guided imagery

She uses therapeutic music activities in groups to reinforce DBT skills which are the subject of this book.

www.therapeuticmusic.net
www.dbtmusic.com

INTRODUCTION

INTRODUCTION

This book presents Therapeutic Music Activities to reinforce and anchor DBT Skills (and other positive life skills) and to assist in the recovery and treatment of issues related to:

Addiction	Interpersonal Effectiveness
Adolescence	Invalidating Environment
Anger	Life
Behavior Problems	Mental health
Being in the System	Mindfulness
Childhood	Self-esteem, self image
Distress Tolerance	Self Expression
Emotion Regulation	Stress
Emotional Vulnerability	Self-Harm
Impulsivity	Suicidal Tendencies
	Trauma

My intent is to print activities in this book that are my original creations. Some of the activities may have had outside origins which I modified, and I want to credit anyone to whom credit is due. I want to thank all those who have contributed in any way to my work, knowingly or unknowingly.

The activities presented are a sampling and are meant to spark your own ideas or to remind you of other activities you already know that you can use to reinforce skills. Feel free to add, subtract, modify, improvise, or change any idea.

You will be given therapeutic value, a list of DBT skills reinforced, materials needed, and instructions for each activity as well as reproducible lyric sheets and guitar chords for the songs. After doing the activity with your group members, use the information to reinforce the skills. Ask group members what DBT skills were practiced in the activity they just did or explain to them what skills they practiced.

The instructions and activities are written in such a way that they can make sense to those of you who have no musical background as well as those who do.

DBT SKILLS SUMMARY

Following is a list of Dialectical Behavioral Therapy skills, summarized from the work of Marsha Linehan.   For more information see the **Skills Training Manual for Treating Borderline Personality Disorder**, The Guilford Press, Copyright 1993.   For DBT resources or training visit http://www.behavioraltech.com/

DBT SKILLS SUMMARY

EMOTION REGULATION SKILLS

1. Thinking rationally instead of irrationally
2. Building Mastery– doing something a little challenging to make yourself feel more competent and in control
3. Increasing positive emotions by doing pleasant things that are possible now
4. Building a life worth living by working on a) long term goals b) repairing or making new relationships c) facing a problem you have been avoiding
5. Staying mindful of positive experiences when mind wanders to the negative
6. Opposite action– changing emotions by acting opposite to the current emotion

DISTRESS TOLERANCE SKILLS

1. Thinking about pros and cons to evaluate my behavior
2. Focusing on breathing, imagery, or half smile
3. Distracting with Wise Mind ACCEPTS: **A**ctivities, **C**ontributing, **C**omparisons, opposite **E**motions, **P**ushing away, other **T**houghts, or **S**ensations
4. Practicing radical acceptance of something from deep within
5. Practicing willingness versus willfulness– willing hands
6. Self soothing: with vision, hearing, smell, taste, and touch
7. IMPROVE the Moment with **I**magery, **M**eaning, **P**rayer, **R**elaxation, focus on **O**ne thing in the moment, brief **V**acation, and self **E**ncouragement

INTERPERSONAL EFFECTIVENESS SKILLS

1. Using DEAR MAN to get what you want– **D**escribe, **E**xpress, **A**ssert, **R**einforce, stay **M**indful, **A**ppear confident, **N**egotiate
2. Adding GIVE when relationship is most important: be **G**entle, act **I**nterested, **V**alidate, and use an **E**asy manner
3. Adding FAST when self respect is most important: Be **F**air, no **A**pologies, **S**tick to your values, be **T**ruthful

CORE MINDFULNESS SKILLS

1. Practicing Wise Mind when dealing with a difficult situation
2. Observing: Teflon mind; noticing thoughts, feelings, and experiences without reacting to them
3. Describing: Putting your experience into words to better understand
4. Participating mindfully with full awareness here and now with undivided attention
5. Being nonjudgmental about yourself and others; focusing on facts, consequences

MUSIC THERAPY

MUSIC THERAPY

As defined by the Certification Board for Music Therapists, "Music therapy is the specialized use of music by a credentialed (music therapy) professional who develops individualized treatment and supportive interventions with people of all ages and ability levels to address social, communication, emotional, physical, cognitive, sensory and spiritual needs."

Therapeutic music sessions are designed for individuals and groups based on client needs. Music therapy interventions include: listening to music, lyric discussion, song writing, music and imagery, playing music, and learning through music. Music therapists participate in interdisciplinary treatment planning, assessment and progress, and follow up.

A music therapist must adhere to the music therapy professional standards of practice and code of ethics and demonstrate competencies as outlined by the American Music Therapy Association and the Certification Board for Music Therapy. Continuing education and re-certification are required to maintain board certification credentials.

You are welcome to use any of the therapeutic music activities in this book; however, the use of any of the resources in this book can NOT be called MUSIC THERAPY unless you are a qualified music therapist.

For more information about music therapy, what it takes to be qualified as a music therapist, or to locate a music therapist, visit www.musictherapy.org.

LISTENING TO MUSIC

LISTENING TO MUSIC: CHOOSE A SONG THAT DESCRIBES YOU

Therapeutic Value:

This listening activity is good for self expression, self exploration and skill application. The same piece of music will affect each person differently, and each person will have a very different interpretation of what the song means to them. Their interpretations are very telling.

DBT Skills that are reinforced:

Core Mindfulness: one-mindfully, non-judgmentally, effectively
Emotion Regulation: mindful of current emotion, increasing positive emotions by doing pleasant things that are possible now
Distress Tolerance: distrac*ting with* Wise Mind ACCEPTS - (activities, contributing, comparisons, thoughts, sensations), self-soothe, one thing in the moment, willingness, IMPROVE *the moment*

Supplies Needed:

A list of songs that the group members can select from and listen to, CDs or iPod with recorded music to play

Instructions:

1. Ask group participants to choose a song that describes something about them. Tell them not to base their choice on the fact that they like the singer or the beat but rather to select one based on the fact that it says something about them.

2. Ask everyone to listen to each selected song and be prepared to share what it means to them.

3. After listening to their song have the person who chose it describe why they chose that song.

4. Next ask the other group members what that song means to them.

5. Finally, ask group members to think about what they would say to a person who is in a situation like the one in the song. What skills would they recommend? What advice would they give the singer of that song? Were there any skills used in the song? What skills could group members use or have they used when faced with similar situations?

Examples of Songs Group Members Chose and Why

- *Perfect* by Simple Plan "because I'm not perfect enough so Dad left me"

Skills they could have used– rational vs. irrational, self-soothe, IMPROVE the moment with self-encouragement.

- *One Step Closer* by Linkin Park "because I feel one step closer to the edge of angry outbursts."

Skills they could have used– self-soothe, imagery, breathing, pros & cons.

- *Time of Your Life* by Green Day "because I want to get through this part of my life and look back and say I had a good life, made good decisions, and got through it and had a good life."

Skills used- increase positive emotions with goal-setting

- *Blue* by Eiffel 65, "because I'm blue."

Skills they could have used– self-soothe, increase positive emotions

LISTENING TO MUSIC: THOUGHTS AND FEELINGS

Therapeutic Value:

This is a good exercise for self expression, emotional release, and for an opportunity to review and reinforce skills.

DBT Skills that are reinforced:

> Core Mindfulness: one-mindfully, non-judgmentally, effectively
> Emotion Regulation: mindful of current emotion, increasing positive emotions by doing pleasant things that are possible now
> Distress Tolerance: distrac*ting* with Wise Mind ACCEPTS - (activities, contributing, comparisons, thoughts, sensations), self-soothe, one thing in the moment, willingness, IMPROVE the moment

Supplies Needed:

CDs or iPod with recorded music to play. Paper, pencils, markers, colors, art supplies, etc.

Instructions:

While listening to music, have the group members write down their feelings and thoughts about each song or even draw to the music.

Follow by sharing and discussion of skills.

Examples:

Hope by Shaggy– "If I didn't have hope when I roll out of bed each morning, I would probably be dead. Never forget that there is always hope."

Arms Wide Open by Creed– "This song made me feel hopeful and think about showing my baby the world."

Oops I Did It Again by Brittany Spears- "So many times I've messed up. I need to realize that I'm not only hurting myself but others, and it hurts to know I'm causing that pain. I've made too many people believe that I'm getting better when, in fact, I'm slowly dying away inside."

Wishing It Was by Santana– "This song makes me feel good. I can relate to it because I always wish things were different. But I am hopeful, and I know things will change and be better."

Kryptonite- "This song is about me and the secrets I keep about my dad"

LISTENING TO MUSIC: LYRIC ANALYSIS

Therapeutic Value:

Lyric analysis involves listening to music with a focus on discussing something about the lyrics afterward. It is great for focusing and for self expression, self exploration, and self disclosure.

DBT Skills that are reinforced:

Core Mindfulness: one-mindfully, nonjudgmentally, observe, describe, participate

Emotion Regulation: rational irrational, increasing positive emotions

Distress Tolerance: distraction (with activities, contributing, comparisons, opposite emotions, pushing away, other thoughts), radical acceptance, willingness, self soothe, IMPROVE the moment (with imagery, meaning, relaxation, one thing in the moment, vacation)

Supplies Needed:

Bring a print out of a song's lyrics and a recording of the song. You can use just about any song the group members like that fits the regulations of your facility... (Some facilities have a pretty strict code of what is appropriate to listen to such as nothing with explicit lyrics, drugs, sex, violence...) You can also print out questions such as those on the following page.

Instructions:

1. Pass out a copy of the lyrics first, if possible.

2. Ask thought provoking questions after.

The following page is an example of lyric analysis done to the song *All Star* by Smash Mouth

ALL STAR by Smash Mouth

So much to do so much to see
So what's wrong with takin the backstreets
You'll never know if you don't go. You'll never shine if you don't glow.

1. What does this mean to you?

2. What is it that you want to accomplish, experience, have, be, or do, yet so far, something has stopped you from trying it?

Hey now, you're an All Star, get your game on, go play

3. What is your game?

Hey now, you're a Rock Star, get the show on, get paid
And all that glitters is gold
Only shooting stars break the mold.

4. Shoot past your own limitations. Dream big. Do it. You CAN do it!! What limiting thought is keeping you from doing it?

Well, the years start coming and they don't stop coming.

5. Time goes by. Are you willing to take a step towards being the glittering star that only you can be and shine? What is the first step for you?

LISTENING TO MUSIC: NAME THAT TUNE/SING THE NEXT LINE

Therapeutic Value:
Teamwork, good sportsmanship, mindfulness, reality orientation, and skill reinforcement

DBT Skills that are reinforced:
Core Mindfulness: one-mindfully, non-judgmentally, effectively

Emotion Regulation: increasing positive emotions by doing pleasant things that are possible now

Distress Tolerance: Distrac*ting* with Wise Mind ACCEPTS - (activities, contributing, comparisons, opposite emotions, thoughts, sensations), self-soothe, one thing in the moment, willingness, IMPROVE the moment (meaning, one thing in the moment, encouragement)

Supplies Needed:
A variety of recorded songs and paper or a white board to keep score

Instructions:
1. Divide into teams.
2. The first team has 30 seconds to name that tune, and then when you stop the music, someone from that team has to sing the next line.
3. After you stop the music and someone sings the next line, play the music again to see if they were correct.
4. It is possible to get 2 points for naming the tune and another 2 points for singing the next line correctly.
5. If team 1 doesn't guess correctly in time, team 2 gets to try for the next 30 seconds on the same song.
6. Regardless of who got the correct answers to the first song, or if no one got them correct, then move on to the next song and it is now team 2s turn. If team 2 doesn't guess correctly in time, team 1 gets to try.

LISTENING TO MUSIC: BINGO

Therapeutic Value:

Paying attention, socialization, reality orienting to here and now

DBT Skills that are reinforced:

Core Mindfulness: one-mindfully, non-judgmentally, effectively

Emotion Regulation: increasing positive emotions by doing pleasant things that are possible now

Distress Tolerance: Distract*ing* with Wise Mind ACCEPTS - (activities, contributing, comparisons, opposite emotions, thoughts), self-soothe, one thing in the moment, willingness, IMPROVE the moment (one thing in the moment, encouragement)

Supplies Needed:

On the next page is a blank bingo game form. Fill in the blanks with song titles that are familiar to the group members. Rearrange the sequence on each bingo card so no one gets bingo at the same time. Bring recordings of each of the songs.

Instructions:

1... Play the songs on the CD player. Play each song for 30 seconds. Players put a marker on their bingo card. Anyone who knows the answer says the answer out loud so that everyone else knows which one to mark.

2... Whoever gets bingo has to read off the titles in the winning row to verify that all the songs were played. Then they get to choose a song to listen to on the CD player listening to the entire song.

3. Another way to play is to give a verbal cue such as "This song was the theme song to a Disney movie," and the group members look on the card and guess "In the Jungle". Whoever guessed correctly first gets to give the next clue. The person giving clues cannot use the title as part of the clue.

B I N G O

SONG WRITING

SONG WRITING:
POSITIVE AFFIRMATIONS

Therapeutic Value: self-expression, reinforcement of skills, teamwork, respect

DBT Skills that are reinforced:

Mindfulness: Non-judgmentally, effectively, observe describe participate, one-mindfully
Interpersonal Effectiveness: DEARMAN, GIVE, FAST
Emotion regulation: build mastery, build positive experiences
Distress Tolerance: distraction-(activities, contributing, comparison, emotions, pushing away, thoughts, sensations) self soothe, IMPROVE, willingness, radical acceptance, Improve the Moment with Imagery, Meaning, Prayer, Relaxation, focus on One thing in the moment, brief Vacation, and self Encouragement

About Affirmations:

Music is a powerful way to anchor thoughts into our subconscious mind. TV ads and radio commercials use jingles that stay in our heads, so we buy whatever they are advertising. What better way to reprogram our subconscious mind with positive affirmations and words of encouragement than to write a song and put the positive lyrics to music!

An affirmation is a positive statement in present tense as if it is happening now.

Thoughts can either limit us or create the results we want. The idea is to become aware of our thoughts and to allow only positive thoughts to dominate our thinking. We will be painting a picture of what we want to be true as if it already is. By telling ourselves we can succeed we can.

Supplies Needed:
Paper, pencils, (karaoke CDs if you have them or want to use them)

Song Writing- POSITIVE AFFIRMATIONS-continued

Instructions:

1. Have group members fill in these blanks:

I deserve____, I am willing to ____, I am learning to ____.

2. Go around the room so they can share what they have written.

3. Ask them how it felt to say the statements. (Positive, encouraging, empowering.)

4. Ask group members to write out 3 negative things they tell themselves. I am ____. And then turn them into positive affirmations. For example: I always make mistakes. I am stupid. I never do anything right. <u>Affirmation:</u> I am getting better every time I do this. I am learning every day. It's okay to make mistakes. Willingness to fail leads to success.

5. Give the direction: "paint a picture in words of how you want things to be for you. You can use the sentences with the filled in blanks or not. This can look like a song, a rap, a paragraph, some sentences describing what you put in those 3 blanks or using other affirmations."

6. You could arrange this as a partner activity.

7. You can offer the use of karaoke CDs for background music when they read or rap their story or poem or song. Some will sing their song without music or will just read it.

Group Members' Song Examples Using Affirmations:

I can get through this because I know I can do anything I put my mind to
I'm good at what I do and I can accomplish whatever I try to
I'm smart and loveable, have faith in myself
I am great, strong, unique unlike anyone else
I work hard learn DBT using skills every day
I handle depression and avoid aggression or oppression, cope well with words I can't say
I'm free, my life is good, I let others in
Communicate, be a success, just got to begin.

I can do it I know that I can
I can go any length with you by my side
I can feel it now, so sure and so true
I'm gonna make it, and to my heart be true.

1.
I strive
I'm determined
Learning the ropes to achieve
I strive
I'm determined
So give me my papers I'm ready to leave.

Chorus:
Because I'm awake and aware now
Determined to succeed
Because I'm awake and aware now
Determined to succeed

2.
I can survive
Stay off the dope
I have
A life
I'm learning now how to really cope.

Chorus:
Because I'm awake and aware now
Determined to succeed
Because I'm awake and aware now
Determined to succeed

3.
I am
Motivated
Exercise makes me elated
I take
My medications
So I don't get agitated

Chorus:
Because I'm awake and aware now
Determined to succeed
Because I'm awake and aware now
Determined to succeed

4.
If I
Stay away
---From drug abuse
I won't go
Waka doodle
Or- knock a screw loose

Chorus:
Because I'm awake and aware now
Determined to succeed
Because I'm awake and aware now
Determined to succeed

5.
To work
Is to Live
To live is to be free
The sweet
Sweet freedom
--of- sobriety.

Chorus:
Because I'm awake and aware now
Determined to succeed
Because I'm awake and aware now
Determined to succeed

SONG WRITING: METAPHORS

Therapeutic Value:

Creative self-expression.

DBT Skills that are reinforced:

Core mindfulness: Non-judgmentally, effectively, observe describe participate, one-mindfully

Emotion regulation: build mastery, build positive experiences

Distress Tolerance: distraction-(activities, contributing, comparison, emotions, pushing away, thoughts, sensations) self soothe, IMPROVE, willingness, radical acceptance, Improve the Moment with Imagery, Meaning, Prayer, Relaxation, focus on One thing in the moment, brief Vacation, and self Encouragement

Supplies Needed:

A list of action words (such as slide, glide, blow, flow, jump, fall) and/or metaphors (such as a sinking ship, a maze, a castle) which group members can use to describe their lives.

Instructions:

1. Pass out the list of action words and/or metaphors and have each person circle any of the words that describe them or that speak to them.
2. Ask them to write sentences describing why they circled those words.
3. Write a song or a rap or a poem or a paragraph from that material.

Group Members' Song Examples Using Metaphors:

"My life reminds me of two different things: A maze and a lonely crowd. A maze because my life takes many turns. Sometimes I find a deer path and sometimes I run into a wall; a lonely crowd because very few people understand what's going on to talk with me yet there are hundreds of people around.

I'm in a maze
Can't find my way out
I turn and turn
I look about
I do not know
From where I came
But surely know
I've got me to blame..."

"My life is like a battlefield
Because every day I live is
A fight to go on
Nobody feels what I feel
So I bite my tongue
And move on."

"My life is like a lonely crowd
Waiting to be heard
Wanting to be loved and understood
Not knowing or realizing
No one really cares."

"My life is like thin ice
For I never know
How long it will be
Before I fall in to all
The hurt and pain I feel"

SONG WRITING: GROUP SONG WRITING

Therapeutic Value:

This is a great way for group members to work together, to each contribute to the whole, to express themselves, to brainstorm, to be heard, to be unique, to be creative.

DBT Skills that are reinforced:

Core mindfulness: Non-judgmentally, effectively, observe describe participate, one-mindfully

Emotion regulation: build mastery, build positive experiences

Distress Tolerance: distraction-(activities, contributing, comparison, emotions, pushing away, thoughts, sensations) self soothe, willingness, radical acceptance, , IMPROVE the Moment with Imagery, Meaning, Prayer, Relaxation, focus on One thing in the moment, brief Vacation, and self Encouragement

Supplies Needed:

White board, markers, paper and pencil

Instructions:

1. Choose a topic to write the song about
2. Ask each person to tell you a line about that topic. Write the lines up on the board, not necessarily in the final order. Edits come later. Write exactly what they say because it is validating.
3. Then edit. Move the lines into the order that the group thinks makes sense. You can change endings to rhyme if you want. It either flows organically or YOU have to do a lot of editing.
4. Ask someone to sing the first line. Ask someone else to sing the next line. The group leader can play guitar chords to give it structure, or a group member can if they play guitar. OR you can leave out this step and just have a great song to read or rap.

Song Examples:

This song was written in a group using the method described above. The topic was DBT. Each group member said a line one after the other. In this case the lines fit pretty much in the order they were given.

DBT's the way I start my day
It helps me out in every single way
Like a broken record it plays in my head
To use my wise mind instead
Playing over and over when my mood sways
I have lots of wonderful days.

Pros and cons, wise mind, just to name a few
I like using these; you should try them, too.

Sadness, anger, misery are all helped effectively with DBT
It's an awesome part of my every day
Tomorrow, forever, and the next day
It helps me always; it's good skills to know
DBT rocks -Hooray!
Hooray!

Song Writing- GROUP SONG WRITING-continued

This song was written on the topic of the Wise Mind Accepts skill:

A is for activities, like sports or read a book

Play your music, write a poem, or maybe you can cook.

C is for contributing, be nice to someone else

Random acts of kindness help us feel good about our self

C is for comparison; I am better now than before

Or look at someone who has it worse and you won't feel as sore

E is opposite emotion like when you are feeling sad

And you watch a movie or read a book so soon you're feeling glad.

P is when you push away the things that feel so bad

You come back later and deal with them when you are not so mad

T is for the thoughts you use to fill up your head

So you're thinking

About other stuff instead

S is for sensations like ice in hand

Go for a run, or take a hot tub, or play in the sand.

SONG WRITING: SELF-EXPRESSION

Therapeutic Value:

Self-expression, creativity.

DBT Skills that are reinforced:

Core mindfulness: Non-judgmentally, effectively, observe describe participate, one-mindfully

Emotion regulation: build mastery, build positive experiences

Distress Tolerance: distraction-(activities, contributing, comparison, emotions, pushing away, thoughts, sensations) self soothe, IMPROVE, willingness, radical acceptance, Improve the Moment with Imagery, Meaning, Prayer, Relaxation, focus on One thing in the moment, brief Vacation, and self Encouragement

Supplies Needed:

Paper and pencils. CD player with CD of meaningful songs such as "You'll Make It Through the Rain!"

Instructions:

1. Listen to a song or two and discuss the lyrics.
2. Pass out paper and pencils and have group members write their own song.
   a. Group members can write entirely original song with their own lyrics and melody
   b. Or they can choose an existing song and re-write the lyrics to be about a topic such as Valentine's Day, Halloween, DBT or whatever you choose.
3. Share.

Group Members' Original Self Expression Songs:

SO DEPRESSED
I'm so depressed
In a rush of stress
Life is a mess
God is putting me to the test
All night I can't rest
I got a broken heart in this chest.

STAND BACK
Stand back, you'll come no further, already you're too deep
The Truth beneath this layer to myself I'll keep
Forget the image; destroy the light, for you will never see this side of me
The truth beneath this layer to myself I'll keep
All these feelings are trapped inside, and that is where they will stay
For the truth beneath this layer to myself I'll keep
Cause once these emotions are released, I'll die without a sound.

STANDING UP TALL
I've been through too many things in my
short life
No one should have to endure this kind of
strife
All I can do is let it all go
I got to learn how to flow.

Standing up tall
I'm learning to be strong inside
I'm standing up tall and feeling pride
Standing up tall
I said I'm learning to be strong inside
I'm standing up tall and feeling pride

Well, I get in trouble doin' things I regret
I don't always use my coping skills yet
I should think before I act and use my wise
mind

Take a deep breath to help me unwind.

Although things are hard if I radically accept
I can practice what I learn until I'm adept
Distracting myself doin' things I enjoy
Helps me get free of those things that
annoy

It doesn't really matter how much I fall
If I pick myself up and stand up tall
If I believe in myself and don't give up hope
And I see myself using new ways to cope

Standing up tall
I'm learning to be strong inside
I'm standing up tall and feeling pride
Standing up tall
I said I'm learning to be strong inside
I'm standing up tall and feeling pride

Example of writing new lyrics to an existing song:

HOLIDAY SONG TO THE TUNE OF JINGLE BELLS

The holidays are near
It's almost Christmas Day
We're learning DBT
Use skills every day

We'll have a big party
Our urges might be strong
We want to get to go to it
We're using pros and cons

DBT, DBT, DBT all day
Self sooth, distraction, willingness
Dear Man to get our way
DBT, DBT, DBTs ok
It keeps us cool so we use wise mind
It's such a better way

We can make it through
Filled with lots of hope
Avoiding aggression
With skills that help us cope

Thinking positive
Letting go of stress
Learning to communicate
and be a great success

DBT, DBT, DBT all day
Self sooth, distraction, willingness
Dear Man to get our way
DBT, DBT, DBTs ok
It keeps us cool so we use wise mind
It's such a better way

MOVEMENT

MOVEMENT ACTIVITY

Therapeutic Value:

This activity is good for Memory, Sequencing, Reality Orientation, Stress Release, Coordination, Group Cohesiveness, Fun, and Self-Expression.

DBT Skills that are reinforced:

Core mindfulness: one thing in the moment, observe, describe and participate, non-judgmentally

Distress Tolerance: ACCEPTS (activities, thoughts), willingness

Emotion Regulation: mastery, build positive emotions, opposite action

Supplies Needed:

Recorded music with a good dance beat.

Instructions:

1. Stand in a circle. One person leads the group in a movement, a simple movement that everyone does together for 4 or 8 beats of the music you play.

2. Then the second person does their movement which everyone copies for the same number of beats.

3. Go back to the first, the second, and then add a third movement.

4. Start from the beginning every time adding each new movement as you move around the circle until everyone has been added into the choreography one at a time. Go around the entire circle.

MAKING MUSIC

MAKING MUSIC: ACTIVITIES FOR MELODIC INSTRUMENTS

Therapeutic Value:

Playing an instrument takes focus, generates feelings of pride, and builds self esteem. The participants, from the low functioning to the conduct disordered or antisocial, pay attention, take turns; wait their turn, focus, and feel good about themselves. They practice being free of judgment of themselves and others. They are distracted from their problems by focusing on the here and now of the music playing. They build mastery by practicing their parts over and over until they learn them. Even if group participants don't know how to play a musical instrument they can be set up for success.

DBT Skills that are reinforced:

Core Mindfulness: one-mindfully, non-judgmentally, effectively
Distress Tolerance: distraction- (activities, contributing, thoughts), self-soothe, one thing in the moment, pros and cons
Emotion Regulation: build mastery

Supplies Needed:

Musical instruments such as keyboards, chimes, guitars, violins, xylophones, a Q-Chord, a mandolin, a steel drum, and so forth

Instructions:

1. Label the keys (or whatever makes the notes) with letters representing the note names.

2. Write out a familiar song or songs using the letters of the note names. (See the sample song sheet on next page.)

3. This could alternately be done with colors by assigning a color to each note. Colored dots from an office supply store work well.

4. Give each group member an instrument and a song sheet and ask them to choose a song or make up an original tune to play for the group by the end of the hour. They each focus on their own activity. It is noisy so be prepared. Instruments with headphones are helpful. Walk around and encourage individuals. After a short time, ask group members to stop and play what they are working on one at a time. You will be impressed.

5. For a group performance that doesn't take much time to rehearse, divide a song into sections and give each participant a section. For example, *The 12 Days of Christmas* can be divided like this:

   Person 1 has the melody for "On the x day of Christmas my true love gave to me"

   Person two has the melody for "a partridge in a pear tree."

   Person three has the melody for "Two turtle doves"

   And so on, with each person taking turns playing their line on cue

AMAZING GRACE

DG BB AG ED

DG BB AD

BD BG DE ED

DG BB AG

MARY HAD A LITTLE LAMB

E D C D E E E D D D E E E

E D C D E E E D D E D C

AMERICA (MY COUNTRY TIS OF THEE)

C C D B C D E E F E D C D C B C

G G G G FE F F F F ED E FEDC E FG

AF E D C

HAPPY BIRTHDAY

GG A G C B

GG A G D C

G G G E C B A

FF E C D C

IN THE JUNGLE

C DE D EF ED C DE D C E D

G ED E GF ED C DE D C E D

MAKING MUSIC: ACTIVITIES FOR DRUMS AND RHYTHM INSTRUMENTS

Therapeutic Value:

It takes mindfulness to play your own rhythm while someone else is playing theirs and to make it sound good. It also takes willingness and some impulse control to not just beat the drum incessantly but to take turns. This is a good forum for self –expression.

DBT Skills that are reinforced:

Emotion Regulation- increase positive emotions, build mastery
Distress Tolerance-distraction (with activities, thoughts, opposite emotion), willingness, self soothing
Core Mindfulness- mindfulness, one thing in the moment

Supplies Needed:

Drums such as Arthur Hull's nesting drums, sound shapes, or paddle drums, and a variety of rhythm instruments such as woodblocks, claves, maracas, tambourines, etc. You can also make rhythm instruments out of coffee cans for drums and toilet paper rolls filled with beans for shakers.

Instructions:

1. Ask group members to name some DBT skills (such as "Wise Mind ACCEPTS, Pros and Cons, DEAR MAN, Willingness"). Clap the names of the skills.

2. Pass out rhythm instruments and drums.

3. Play the rhythms of the skill names together as a group. For example, say "Wise Mind ACCEPTS", then echo on the instruments several times. Take turns leading, having each group member state a skill name and the group echoing the rhythm of it on their instruments.

4. Make up affirmations, positive words of encouragement such as "I can do It, I know that I can," and play the rhythm of that on the drum. Take turns around the circle.

5. Divide into groups and assign a different rhythm to each group. It takes mindfulness to focus on your own rhythm. For example group 1 plays "pros and cons (rest)" and group 2 plays "wise mind accepts (rest)" starting on "cons" so "cons" and "wise" happen together.

6. Another way to drum using DBT skills is to have someone start and keep a steady beat and ask the group members to mindfully listen. Their task is to create balance between sound and silence. Allow them to improvise, and to play whatever they feel like playing on their instrument but to listen for the silence in-between the sounds. "If it doesn't sound good, stop and listen, then start again."

7. Have one group of instruments play while the others listen, taking turns. Just the wooden instruments, or just the shaken instruments, or just the drums. This takes impulse control. Then go back to everyone playing together.

8. Pair up people and have them play together as partners without communicating about it first with words. Just make it sound good by listening mindfully.

9. DBT rap or rhythm- Group members can make up a rap to use for rhythms. Here is a DBT rhythm for pros and cons.

(Part 1)

Pros and Cons
Pros and Cons
(Part 2)
Think about the consequences when I feel my urges
Think about the consequences when I feel my urges
(Part 3)
Stop,(rest), and Think
Stop, (rest), and Think (The word "rest" is not spoken, it is a silent beat"

The lyrics of this song can be found in reproducible format in the SONGS section of this book along with further instructions for use. It is one of the songs on the "You'll Make It Through the Rain! " CD

MAKING MUSIC: RHYTHM ACTIVITY- NO INSTRUMENTS

(I don't know where I learned this, so I apologize for not crediting the source.)

Therapeutic Value:

This activity takes mindfulness, paying attention, focus. It is an activity which can distract us from whatever is happening with us emotionally. It can create opposite emotions.

DBT Skills that are reinforced:
Distress Tolerance: distraction-(activity, thoughts, opposite emotion) willingness, radical acceptance.
Core Mindfulness: one thing in the moment, one mindfully

Instructions:

1. Count off so that each person around a circle has a number.

2. Keep a steady quarter note rhythm using your body: Hands on knees twice, clap hands together twice, and snap fingers once on each hand.

3. The first person calls his own number on the first snap and then calls the number of the next person in the circle on the second snap.

4. Go in order until everyone understands: First, person number 1 calls out "one-two"; then person number 2 calls out "two-three", and so on for however many there are in the circle.

5. Once they have gone around the circle and all have done it correctly, then instruct them to call their own number on the first snap and any other persons number on the second snap. (i.e. 1-6, 6-5, 5-8...) The person whose number is called on the second snap takes the next turn.

6. Once everyone has mastered it, he who hesitates or makes a mistake is out.

7. This can be varied by using people's names.

MAKING MUSIC: SINGING KARAOKE

Therapeutic Value:

Karaoke is an easy, fairly inexpensive way for a group to have a sing along where all are involved. It's nice that the lyrics can be viewed on the TV screen for all to see. This activity fosters self-expression, group cohesion, and fun. It changes people's moods.

DBT Skills that are reinforced:
Core Mindfulness: one-mindfully, non-judgmentally, effectively
Distress Tolerance: distraction with Wise Mind ACCEPTS (activities, contributing, comparison, opposite emotions, push away, thoughts), self-soothe, one thing in the moment, pros and cons
Emotion Regulation: build mastery, opposite action, increasing positive emotions

Supplies Needed:

A karaoke machine, karaoke CDs, a microphone, and a booklet of available songs that group members can select a song from

Instructions:

Set up some karaoke rules: Respect each other. Don't laugh at the singer or make fun of the song that was selected. Don't talk during the song. Practice being non-judgmental.

Each person will get a chance to select a song. When it's someone's turn that person can decide whether they want to sing alone on the microphone or sing all together as a group.

GUIDED IMAGERY

GUIDED IMAGERY

3 goals for using imagery:	DBT Skills Reinforced:
1. Relaxation And Stress Relief	*Distress Tolerance: Imagery, Breathing*
2. Connecting With The Wise Mind	*Core mindfulness: Wise Mind*
3. Rehearsal/ Practicing Being Successful "What You Conceive And Believe You Can Achieve"	*Emotion Regulation: Building Mastery, Accumulating Positives*

Instructions:

I call my imagery group "Inner Harmony."

Ask group members to define the word harmony. "Peace" is the basic answer. In music, it's when the notes blend well and the sounds complement one another.

The way I see it, how can there be peace in the world if there isn't peace within myself first.

Tell group members that in this group they will learn a skill that may help them experience inner harmony and that they can use on their own if it works for them.

Ask questions related to the goal of the group.

- For goal one, ask: "On a scale of 1-100 how stressed do you feel right now?"
- For goals two and three, ask each group member: "If I gave you a magic wand and you could change anything in your life so that you would never have to come back to a place like this, what behavior would you change?" They might answer: "my anger" or "not cutting on myself".
- For goal three ask: "What would you like to be successful at?" or, "What is your dream?"

Talk about the power of imagery

- A prisoner of war who was in solitary confinement for 5 years. During that time, he practiced his golf swing and imagined winning the world golf championship. When he was released guess what happened? He won the golf championship.
- There were two basketball teams; one team practiced shooting hoops every night on the courts while the other just imagined shooting hoops and making the baskets. Who do you think won when they played each other? The team that imagined shooting hoops.

"What we conceive and believe we can achieve. Think about what you want to create for yourself, and we will practice it."

Ask them to share at the beginning and after the imagery experience.

GUIDED IMAGERY: RELAXATION & STRESS RELIEF

Music:

Relaxing music. I play Garden of Serenity by Steve Gordon, Sequoia Records

Suggestion Script:

Sit comfortably and allow yourself to focus on your breath. Every time you breathe in, feel peace and relaxation entering your body; and every time you breathe out, feel stress and tension leaving your body. Breathe in peace and relaxation, and breathe out tension and stress.

Perhaps your relaxing breath has a color to it. Notice the color of relaxation and peace. Feel the color of relaxation and peace as it touches all the parts of your body with your in-breaths. Notice how good it feels.

Notice the color of stress and tension as it leaves your body.

Feel the relaxing breaths fill your body with peace and allow that relaxing color to wash out the stress and tension. Release the stress and tension on the out-breaths. Continue to breathe in peace and relaxation and breathe out stress and tension.

You might find that that this process continues on its own as you continue to breath normally throughout the rest of the (day or) night. You might find that just from breathing normally and naturally that your body begins to feel more relaxed and you feel a sense of peace inside. You might even notice that some of your feelings of stress and tension simply melt away.

And anytime you feel an urge to act out upon your impulses, you can find it easy to take a deep breath and feel the same relaxed peaceful feeling you feel right now. You can find it easy to make wise choices about your behaviors. And any time you think about a stress producing thought, you can find it easy to breathe in relaxation and breathe out the stress, allowing yourself to enjoy a peaceful stress free (day or) night.

And you can practice that right now. Imagine being in a situation where in the past you might have felt like acting out impulsively. Imagine being in that situation now and taking a deep relaxing breath. Notice how easily you can breathe out the urge and find yourself acting wisely.

Any time you think about a stress producing thought, you can find it easy to breathe in relaxation and breathe out the stress, allowing yourself to enjoy a peaceful stress free time.

Now notice yourself in a situation where in the past you had felt stressed about something. Imagine breathing in relaxation and peace, and breathing out the stress, finding it easy to let go of the stressful feelings.

I am going to ask you to continue breathing in peace and relaxation and breathing out stress and tension. And as I turn down the music, you can bring your awareness back into this room, opening your eyes, relaxed and stress free.

GUIDED IMAGERY-WISE ONE JOURNEY

Music:

Relaxing music. I play "Sacred Earth Drums" by Steve Gordon, Sequoia Records

Suggestion Script:

We are going to go on an imaginary journey to meet your inner wise one, who may be a person, or may be an animal. Whatever form your wise one takes today, you will be able to ask questions and receive answers. You will be able to gain awareness of how to connect with your wise one when you want to. You will be more in touch with your own wise mind, your inner knowing and intuition.

Make yourself comfortable. You can close your eyes or keep them open. As you hear the sound of the music and the sound of my voice, you can begin to relax, knowing that you can make any adjustments at any time to be comfortable.

Imagine waves of relaxing energy flowing through your body. Invite these waves of relaxation to move in through the top of your head, relaxing your scalp, relaxing your eyes and your cheeks and your jaw. You might notice if the relaxing energy has a color, and notice how it feels as it reaches all the different parts of your body. And as these waves of relaxing energy move down further into your body, you can find it easy to relax your neck muscles, relaxing your shoulders and your arms all the way down to your fingertips. With every breath you take you can relax even deeper inside. Allow these relaxing waves of energy to move down your back where any stress or tension can easily melt away. And now, you can invite these waves of relaxation to move down from your waist to your hips, and from your hips down your legs all the way down to the bottom of your feet... From the top of your head to the bottom of your feet, your body has nothing to do now but relax and let go.

Imagine walking in a natural place. You can feel your feet touching the ground. You can feel the temperature of the air on your skin. You can hear the sounds of nature all around you.

You can smell the scent of the outdoor air. You can see whatever there is to see in your natural place. Allow the music to take you to a place that feels very safe and very good to you. Feel just how good it feels to be in your own special and safe place.

And in your safe and special place today, perhaps you can begin to sense the presence of a wise one here with you. Your wise one might be a person or it might be an animal. Whichever it is, your wise one feels very safe and very wise and has a message for you today that can help you in your life.   Notice what the message is. Spend some time asking questions and receiving answers from your inner wise one. (pause)

You can connect with your inner wise one anytime you want to or need to, easily.   You can remember everything you want to remember about your experience today. You can return easily to this place in your inner world whenever you want to. And as you breathe, begin to bring your awareness back to being in a room filled with people. As I turn down the music and count from one to five you can come back into the room here feeling alert, awake, and alive.

Examples:

A group member who is suicidal: "My wise one was a goddess and the message was 'live. ' Whenever I feel dead and cold, I know exactly where to go now."

A group member who wanted to handle anger in new ways: "That was awesome! I feel like I've got an avenue for handling my anger. I have a place to go to calm down. I will use it whenever I feel like hanging myself."

A group member who wanted to deal with his anger: "When I feel depressed, I can go there and be undepressed. If I'm mad, I can go there. My message was on how to keep out of trouble and accomplish what I want."

"This was my message: 'Only by walking through the shadows can one come through to the light. Never stop trying; you can always turn around your life.'"

GUIDED IMAGERY: SUCCESS

Music:

Relaxing music. I play "Sacred Earth Drums" by Steve Gordon

Suggestion Script:

Today you will have a chance to practice being successful at whatever your dream is. Maybe it's handling your anger in new ways. Maybe it's learning a new way to deal with your urge to hurt yourself. Maybe it's being successful at being a professional of some sort: a doctor or a veterinarian or a teacher or a crime scene investigator. Maybe it has to do with getting along better with someone, getting a job, doing well at school. Think about what your dream is, and you will now have an opportunity to experience being successful at that.

 Make yourself comfortable. You can close your eyes or keep them open. As you hear the sound of the music and the sound of my voice, you can begin to relax, knowing that you can make any adjustments at any time to be comfortable.

 Imagine waves of relaxing energy flowing through your body. You can invite these waves of relaxation to move in through the top of your head, relaxing your scalp, relaxing your eyes and your cheeks and your jaw. And as these waves of relaxing energy move down further down your body, you can find it easy to relax your neck muscles, relaxing your shoulders and your arms all the way down to your fingertips. With every breath you take you can relax even deeper inside.   Allow these relaxing waves of energy to move down your back where any stress or tension can easily melt away. And now, you can invite these waves of relaxation to move down from your waist to your hips, and from your hips all the way down your legs to the bottom of your feet... From the top of your head to the bottom of your feet, your body has nothing to do now but relax and let go.

Imagine walking in a natural place. You can feel your feet touching the ground. You can feel the temperature of the air on your skin. You can hear the sounds of nature all around you.

You can smell the scent of the outdoor air. You can see whatever there is to see in your natural place. Allow the music to take you to a place that feels very safe and very good to you. Feel just how good it feels to be in your own special and safe place.

And in your safe and special place today, perhaps you can begin to sense the presence of a wise one here with you. Your wise one might be a person or it might be an animal. Whichever it is, your wise one feels very safe and very wise and has a message for you today that can help you in your life. Notice what the message is. Spend some time asking questions and receiving answers from your inner wise one. (pause)

And now allow your wise one to take you into the future to see the future successful you. The future you who has already learned a new way to handle your anger, or the you who is free of all self-harming behaviors. The you who has already succeeded at whatever it is you said you wanted to succeed at when you were asked at the beginning of this group. Become that future successful you now, and feel what it feels like to have accomplished your goal. Notice how it feels in your body. Notice how you are acting, what you are doing differently. Notice the people around you, what you are wearing, and all the details you can notice. (pause) And any time you think of this goal, you can remember how it feels to have already accomplished it, and you can find it easy to achieve it.

Now once again find yourself with your wise on in your own safe /special place, as your present day self. You can talk to your wise one, perhaps asking about the best way for you to get from where you are now to where you want to be to succeed.

Know that you can easily remember everything you want to remember about your journey here today. You can return easily to this place in your inner world whenever you want to. You can connect with your inner wise person whenever you need to. And as you breathe, begin to bring your awareness back to being in the room filled with people. As I turn down the music and count from one to five, you can come back into the room, feeling alert, awake, and alive.

Example:

A group member who wanted to take the steps to achieve her goals but felt that something was in the way:

"I was at my special place where the rock formation in the woods is when my bear wise being came to me and told me 'It's storming now, but you'll make it through the rain.' He took me into the future and let me see myself in a black outfit with a microphone on stage speaking to the people as a motivational speaker. And I told myself that I know what I gotta do– stay goal oriented and one day I'll be there."

(This one was the inspiration for the song "I'm Gonna Make It "featured on the "You'll Make it Through the Rain" CD.)

SONGS

You'll Make It Through the Rain!

The following 5 songs are on the CD "You'll Make It Through the Rain!"

The Roller Coaster Ride
The Message
The System
I'm Gonna Make It
Pros and Cons

Included here are instructions, reproducible lyric sheets, and guitar chords for each song. Permission to reproduce lyric sheets for therapeutic use is granted.

For information about purchasing the CD see the resource page at the end of this book.

THE ROLLER COASTER RIDE

Therapeutic Value:

This song reinforces alternatives to acting out on anger. It teaches how to gain self awareness and to bring oneself into wise mind when on the road to impulsivity. It exemplifies mindfulness. It reinforces the idea that it's not too late to stop and think.

DBT Skills that are reinforced:

Core mindfulness: emotion mind, wise mind, observe, describe and participate
Distress Tolerance: ACCEPTS (activities, thoughts), willingness, self soothe
Emotion Regulation: build positive emotions

When we get overwhelmed by our emotions there is a point of no return (Roller Coaster) where we act impulsively, reactively, instinctively, without any thought of consequences, and we don't even care. How can we get out of the grip of our emotions and make a wise choice about our behavior that won't leave us regretting something we did?

Instructions:

Before playing the song, ask group members to listen for the DBT skills that are in the song. After listening, go through the lyric sheet &/or listen again and stop the music in the following places:

1. After the first verse, ask "What mind am I in?" (Emotional)

2. After the first chorus, ask "What does this mean? (I know I'm overwhelmed by my emotions right now; that I feel urges to act out and I don't care, but it's not too late to choose wisely)

3. After the 2nd verse, ask "What is this verse telling us?" (I'm noticing what's happening with me- observing and describing. This gets me out of the grip of emotions. Then I'm able to choose a wise behavior to take care of myself, and I participate effectively.)

The Roller Coaster Ride continued

4. After the 3rd verse, ask "What else could I do that would be wise?" (If you're playing this on the guitar you can sing their answers into the song.) "What skills have we used here? (Distraction, or build positive emotions, or self soothe...)

Responses to This Song:

"I wish I had heard this song before I had my family visit. I would have handled things differently."

"Yeah, I wish I had heard it before too. If I'd heard the Roller Coaster Ride song before I acted out that night it would have gotten me to think twice before I did. Hopefully, before I go off ever, I can recite this song in my head."

The Roller Coaster Ride

Copyright 2007 Deborah Spiegel MT-BC

Somebody treated me unfair
I know I really shouldn't care
But I feel like doing something mean
I don't care if it's right or wrong

Oh, here comes the roller coaster ride
I feel the anger swell inside
It's not too late
To be wise

So emotions don't control me
I notice what's happening with me
Hot tears rolling down my face
My heart's beginning to race
My thoughts are those of revenge
Maybe I should relax with my friends instead

Oh, here comes the roller coaster ride
I feel the anger swell inside
It's not too late
To be wise

Maybe I should go ride my bike
Or I could go for a hike
Walk outside and listen to the brook
I could read a good book…
Run real fast until the anger's gone
Or play guitar and sing you a song

Oh, here comes the roller coaster ride
I feel the anger swell inside
It's not too late
To be wise
It's not too late
To be wise

The Roller Coaster Ride

Copyright 2007 Deborah Spiegel MT-BC

G   C   G
Somebody treated me unfair
G   C   G
I know I really shouldn't care
D   G
But I feel like doing something mean
D   C   G
I don't care if it's right or wrong

G   C   G
Oh, here comes the roller coaster ride
G   C   G
I feel the anger swell inside
D   G
It's not too late
D   G
To be wise

G   C   G
So emotions don't control me
G   C   G
I notice what's happening with me
D   G
Hot tears rolling down my face
D   G
My heart's beginning to race
D   G
My thoughts are those of revenge
D   C
Maybe I should relax with my friends
G
instead

G   C   G
Oh, here comes the roller coaster ride
G   C   G
I feel the anger swell inside
D   G
It's not too late
D   G
To be wise

G   C   G
Maybe I should go ride my bike
G   C   G
Or I could go for a hike
D   G
Walk outside and listen to the brook
D   G
I could read a good book...
D   G
(add your own lines here)
D   G
Run real fast until the anger's gone
D   C   G
Or play guitar and sing you a song

G   C   G
Oh, here comes the roller coaster ride
G   C   G
I feel the anger swell inside
D   G
It's not too late
D   G
To be wise
D   G
It's not too late
D   G
To be wise

THE MESSAGE

Therapeutic Value:

This song starts out by validating the experience of those who feel they are in very hopeless situations and/or who self-harm in any way. (This can include overeating, drinking, impulsive shopping, etc. as well as actually cutting or suicidal behavior) It then offers skills for change or resolution. It was written with the idea of meeting the listeners where they are and then leading them to where they could be. Positive words of encouragement and affirmations are repeated throughout the song in order to plant them in the listeners' subconscious mind and to teach self encouragement and cheerleading.

DBT Skills that are reinforced:

Core mindfulness: wise mind, Teflon mind, nonjudgmental
Distress Tolerance: Pros and cons, ACCEPTS, willingness, self encouragement
Emotion Regulation: thinking rationally, increase positive emotions, mindfully staying positive when mind wanders to the negative, opposite action

Instructions:

1. Instruct group members to listen mindfully to this song as they will be asked which part is their favorite.

2. After listening to this song, ask the group members which of the lines feel the best for them to hear.

3. Discuss the skill of positive encouragement that we give ourselves.

4. Group members can save the lyrics sheets and underline the lyrics that are meaningful to them.

Responses to This Song:

- "This song really moves me. It helps me out a lot. I wish I could listen to it every day because I really think it would change my life and the way I think about myself." "Can I keep the lyrics? Will you bring me a copy of the CD?"

- "I like the line 'She wanted to self harm, not knowing of her charm' because other people see my charm but not the problems I feel inside."

- "I like the line 'She tried to get rid of the pain she felt inside' because it explains me and it makes me feel good to know somebody else feels the same".

- "I like 'When your mind is set, there's nothing you can't do' because it makes me feel like I can do anything if I put my mind to it.

- "I like 'You deserve the best, you can make it through the rest, you're special and you really ought to know.' I want to feel special and I do deserve the best."

The Message

Song written by Deborah Spiegel MT-BC
Board Certified Music Therapist
Copyright 2006

Her life was such a mess
It put her to the test
She didn't really want to live the rest

They weren't always there
She wasn't treated fair
They didn't tell her sweet things good to hear

She wanted to self-harm
Not knowing of her charm
She tried to get rid of the pain she felt inside

It was one deep dark night
When she first saw the light
These words began to swim within her head.

And they said:

CHORUS;
You deserve the best
You can make it through the rest
You're special and you really ought to know

Keep on being you
The way you know to do
Uniquely you is just the way to be

Go the extra mile
Live your life in style
When your mind is set, there's nothing you can't do

Do what you know is right

Keep your goals in sight
Be everything you know that you can be

But her life was oh so blue
She didn't know what else to do
So she told herself these words to help her through:

CHORUS:
You deserve the best
You can make it through the rest
You're special and you really ought to know

Keep on being you
The way you know to do
Uniquely you is just the way to be

Go the extra mile
Live your life in style
When your mind is set, there's nothing you can't do

Do what you know is right
Keep your goals in sight
Be everything you know that you can be

So whenever she was blue
And she didn't know what to do
She'd tell herself things to help her through:

CHORUS:
You deserve the best
You can make it through the rest...

The Message

Song written by Deborah Spiegel MT-BC

Copyright 2006

```
A                    E
Her life was such a mess
A                    E
It put her to the test
A              E      A E
She didn't really want to live the rest



D                A
They weren't always there
D                A
She wasn't treated fair
D                A
They didn't tell her sweet things good to
E
hear



A                E
She wanted to self-harm
A                E
Not knowing of her charm
A                E
She tried to get rid of the pain she felt
A E
inside



D                    A
It was one deep dark night
D                    A
When she first saw the light
D                        A
These words began to swim within her
E
head.



E
And they said:
```

```
CHORUS:
A                D
You deserve the best
E                A
You can make it through the rest
D                  E          A
You're special and you really ought to know
A                D
Keep on being you
E                A
The way you know to do
D            E          A
Uniquely you is just the way to be


A                    D
Go the extra mile
E        A
Live your life in style
D                        E
When your mind is set, there's nothing you
A
can't do


A                    D
Do what you know is right
E              A
Keep your goals in sight
D                    E          A
Be everything you know that you can be…



A                    E
But her life was oh so blue
A                    E
She didn't know what else to do
A                        E
So she told herself these words to help her
A
Through


CHORUS
```

THE SYSTEM SONG

Therapeutic Value:

This song validates the experiences of those who feel trapped in the system. It offers hope and an opportunity to discuss skills.

DBT Skills that are reinforced:

> Core mindfulness: wise mind, observe, describe, and participate
> Distress Tolerance: willingness, IMPROVE the moment with imagery, brief vacation, self encouragement
> Emotion Regulation: rational versus irrational, build positive emotions by working on a long term goal,

Instructions:

1. Listen to the song

2. Ask for listeners' reactions to the song

3. Discuss skills for coping with the situation

4. Ask each group member "what is your dream?"

5. Encourage them to hang in there. "Hold onto your dream and believe. You too can accomplish your dream."

The System Song

by Deborah Spiegel MT-BC, Board-Certified Music Therapist
Copyright 2006

He said I miss my mom
And I miss my dad
And I miss my brothers too
It makes me sad, so I act bad
Doing things I shouldn't do
Deep inside, where he cried
He longed to belong to someone too
He longed to belong to someone too

Trapped in the system with
all kinds of folks
This boy has seen a lot
more than most
Trapped in the system with
all kinds of folks
This boy has seen a lot
more than most

He said I miss my Mom
And I miss my Dad
And I miss my brothers too
It makes me sad, don't wanna act bad
Doing things I shouldn't do
Deep inside, where he cried
He longed to belong to someone too
He longed to belong to someone too

Working the system
He does his best

To gain an hour of freedom
to call his own
Working the system
He tries his best
To gain a minute of freedom
to call his own

He said I miss my mom
And I miss my dad
And I miss my brothers too
It makes me sad, but I don't act bad
Doing things I shouldn't do
Deep inside, where he cried
He longed to belong to someone too
He longed to belong to someone too

He has strength
and he never let go
Held onto his dream and believed
He has strength
and he never let go
Achieved the dream he conceived
Achieved the dream he conceived

The System Song

by Deborah Spiegel MT-BC, Board-Certified Music Therapist
copyright 2006

Chorus:

G
He said I miss my mom
D
And I miss my dad
C   G
And I miss my brothers too
G   D
It makes me sad, so I act bad
        C   G
Doing things I shouldn't do
C   G
Deep inside, where he cried
C   D   C
He longed to belong to someone too
D   CG
He longed to belong to someone too

Verse1:

G   C
Trapped in the system with
F   D
all kinds of folks
G   C
This boy has seen a lot
D   G
more than most
G   C
Trapped in the system with
F   D
all kinds of folks
G   C
This boy has seen a lot
D   G
more than most

Chorus

Verse 2:

G   C
Working the system
F   D
 he does his best
G   C
To gain an hour of freedom
D   G
to call his own
G   C
Working the system
 F   D
he tries his best
G   C
To gain a minute of freedom
D   G
to call his own

Chorus

Verse 3:

G   C
He has strength
F   D
and he never let go
G   C   D
Held onto his dream and believed
G   C
He has strength
F   D
and he never let go
G   C   DG
Achieved the dream he conceived
Achieved the dream he conceived

I'M GONNA MAKE IT!

Therapeutic Value:

This is an uplifting metaphorical song about following your heart. It illustrates positive thinking, cheerleading, opposite action, and self encouragement.

DBT Skills that are reinforced:

Core mindfulness: wise mind

Distress Tolerance: imagery, willingness, IMPROVE the moment with Imagery, self-encouragement

Emotion Regulation: building mastery, building positives by working on a long term goal and facing a problem instead of avoiding

Instructions:

1. Ask group members to listen to the song with their focus on what therapeutic skills they find in it

2. After listening, discuss what the listeners found to be therapeutic about the song and any coping skills they recognized. (Cheerleading, opposite action, encouragement, imagery...)

3. Ask them: "I want to take the steps to reach my goals, but I'm afraid." "Do what your heart tells you to do. Do what you know is best for you." What would you be doing if you followed your heart? What are the steps you want to take to reach your goals?

I'm Gonna Make It!

Song by Deborah Spiegel MT-BC
Copyright 2006

I want to take the steps to reach my goals
But I'm afraid
All my life I've done what I've done
It's hard to change my ways

She was at her special place
By the rocks in the woods
When the bear
Came into view
She could have sworn that he told her what
to do...

He said "It's storming now but you'll make it
through the rain.
You're strong and you deserve to be free of
the pain.
Just follow your heart and know that I'm
here with you
I'll stay by your side and help you make it
through.

And she cried:
I can do it!
I know that I can
I can go any length
With you by my side
I can feel it now
So sure and so true
I'm gonna make it
and to my heart be true

I can do it!
I know that I can
I can go any length
With you by my side
I can feel it now
So sure and so true
I'm gonna make it and to my heart be true

She was watchin' all the birds
And felt the spray of the waterfall
She spied a butterfly purple and blue
It said, "Do what your heart tells you to do.
Do what you know is the best for you."

It said "I was a caterpillar
Crawling on the ground
I followed my heart
And cocooned all around
Now I can fly free and reach to any height
Remember everything will be all right"

And she cried:
I can do it!
I know that I can.
I can soar to any height
Just like you butterfly.
I can feel it now
So sure and so true
I'm gonna make it
and to my heart be true

I can do it!
I know that I can
I can soar to any height
Just like you butterfly
I can feel it now
So sure and so true
I'm gonna make it
and to my heart be true

Yes I'm gonna make it
and to my heart be true.

I'm Gonna Make It!

Song by Deborah Spiegel MT-BC

Copyright 2006

```
C              F            C
I want to take the steps to reach my goals
C        G      C
But I'm afraid
C              F            C
All my life I've done what I've done
C            G        C
It's hard to change my ways


C
She was at her special place
F            C
By the rocks in the woods

When the bear
             G
Came into view
C      F      C
                C        G
She could have sworn that he told her what
 C
to do...


C                                F
He said "It's storming now but you'll make
              C
it through the rain.
C                              G
You're strong and you deserve to be free of the
pain.
C                              F
Just follow your heart and know that I'm
             C
here with you
C                          G
I'll stay by your side and help you make it
 C
through.
```

```
And she cried:
C
I can do it!
F              C
I know that I can
C
I can go any length
G
With you by my side
              C
I can feel it now
              F      C
So sure and so true
C
I'm gonna make it
              G          C
and to my heart be true


C
I can do it!
F                  C
I know that I can
C
I can go any length
G
With you by my side
              C
I can feel it now
              F      C
So sure and so true
C
I'm gonna make it
              G          C
and to my heart be true
```

Deborah Spiegel MT-BC

78

C
She was watchin' all the birds
F   C
And felt the spray of the waterfall
C   G
She spied a butterfly purple and blue
       C   F   C
It said, "Do what your heart tells you to do.
C   G   C
Do what you know is the best for you."

C
It said "I was a caterpillar
F   C
Crawling on the ground
C
I followed my heart
G
And cocooned all around
C   F   C
Now I can fly free and reach to any height
C   G   C
Remember everything will be all right"

And she cried:
C
I can do it!
F   C
I know that I can
C
I can soar to any height

G
Just like you butterfly

         C
I can feel it now
      F   C
So sure and so true
C
I'm gonna make it
        G   C
and to my heart be true

C
I can do it!
F   C
I know that I can
C
I can soar to any height
G
Just like you butterfly
         C
I can feel it now
      F   C
So sure and so true
C
I'm gonna make it
        G   C
and to my heart be true

        C
Yes I'm gonna make it
G   C
and to my heart be true.

PROS & CONS

Therapeutic Value:

It takes mindfulness to focus on your own part and hearing the whole. Many people say that this song gets stuck in their heads and reminds them to stop and think.

DBT Skills that are reinforced:

       Core mindfulness: mindfulness, one thing in the moment
       Distress Tolerance: pros and cons, willingness, distracting with activities and other thoughts or sensations
       Emotion Regulation: build mastery, increase positive emotions, opposite action

Here are the three parts for this song:

     A.   Pros and cons
          Pros and cons

     B.   Think about the consequences when I feel my urges

          Think about the consequences when I feel my urges

     C.   Stop   and think

          Stop   and think

Instructions:

1. Listen to the Pros & Cons song on the CD

2. Read all the lines together out loud as a group

3. Divide the group into three parts and assign one part to each group

4. Tell group members to focus their attention on their part, their group, and how the parts fit together.

5. Group A says their line over and over

6. After 4 repetitions of group A's lines, group B starts their part

7. After 4 repetitions of group B's part group C starts their part

8. After several rounds signal group A to stop

9. Signal group B to stop

10. Signal group C to stop

11. Introduce body rhythms for each group such as:
    a. Foot stomp on beats 1 and 3 for group A: "Pros" (along with foot) "cons" (along with foot)
    b. Slap thighs on each beat 1234 for group B: Think (with slap) bout (with slap) con (with slap) quen (with slap) when (with slap) feel (with slap) urge (with slap) es (with slap)
    c. Clap on beats 2 and 4 for group C: "Stop (then clap) and think (then clap)"

12. Make up a combination of the above using words and/or body rhythms. Say the words or just use the body rhythms. You can have one group say the words while the other groups do their body rhythms and then switch.

Pros and Cons

By Deborah Spiegel MT-BC
Board Certified Music Therapist
Copyright 2005

Pros and cons

Pros and cons

Think about the consequences when I feel my urges

Think about the consequences when I feel my urges

Stop   and think

Stop   and think

RESOURCES

RESOURCES

Dialectical Behavioral Therapy... www.behavioraltech.com

Music Therapy... www.musictherapy.org

Karaoke... www.acekaraoke.com

Music Flashcards ... www.notesnstrings.com

Deborah Spiegel... www.dbtmusic.com or email deborah@dbtmusic.com

To Purchase a Copy of the "You'll Make It Through the Rain" CD:

1. CD Baby has the CD in both downloadable MP3 format as well as physical CD-R format which they will send in the mail.

http://www.cdbaby.com/cd/deborahspiegelmtbc#

2. iTunes has the songs in downloadable format :

http://phobos.apple.com/WebObjects/MZStore.woa/wa/viewAlbum?playListId=276010861

To Purchase a Copy of a Guided Imagery CD containing the 3 suggestion Scripts in this book:

Check on the website www.dbtmusic.com or www.therapeuticmusic.net

Visit the above websites occasionally for updates and new resources.

CPSIA information can be obtained
at www.ICGtesting.com
Printed in the USA
LVHW101511160120
643872LV00002B/24